TRIBAL INFLUENCE

By Ron Vietti

Tribal Influence
Copyright © 2014 by nCourage Media, LLC

Unless otherwise noted all scripture quotations are from the New American Standard Bible, Copyright © 1971, 1995.
Lockman Foundation. Used by permission.
All rights reserved.

No part of this book may be reproduced in any form without permission in writing from the publisher, except in the case of brief quotations embodied in articles or reviews.

Excerpt included taken from **Just Walk Across the Room** by BILL HYBELS. Copyright © 2006 Bill Hybels.
Used by permission by Zondervan.
www.zondervan.com

Published by nCourage Media, LLC
www.ncouragemedia.com
ISBN: 978-0-9914746-1-5
e-book ISBN: 978-0-9914746-0-8
Printed in the United States of America.

ACKNOWLEDGEMENTS

I wanted to say a short thank you to my son, Josh, for suggesting that I write this book. I would not have done it without his input and encouragement. I also want to say thank you to my awesome family for all the support they give me when I spend part of my vacation writing. I would like to give a shout-out to my wife, Debbie, and my lovely grandkids, Joe, Kylee and Kenzee, and my daughter, Tara, for having them. I also want to say thanks to my daughter-in-law, Ashley, and my son-in-law, Jim, for being the best and making our family complete. I couldn't have completed any of this without the help of both my assistant, Nicole Dickey, and my daughter, Tara Crews. My whole staff has been really supportive of me taking time off, and I want to thank them all for covering the bases for me, as I have spent time writing this short-read book. You all deserve a big THANK YOU!

CONTENTS

INTRODUCTION 7

PART 1 HUMAN 11
1. The Need to Belong — 13
2. Sense of Purpose — 21
3. The Power of Connection — 31

PART 2 TRIBAL 41
4. Tribes — 43
5. Tribal Association Beginnings — 59
6. Tribal Fellowship — 67

PART 3 INFLUENCE 73
7. Narrow-Mindedness — 75
8. Spirit of Pride — 87
9. Learning From One Another — 93

PART 4 YOU 103
10. What to Look For in a Tribe — 105
11. Reaching Out and Bridging the Gap — 113
12. The Three Levels of Tribes — 119
13. Making the World a Better Place — 129

INTRODUCTION

I have used the word "tribes" for years to reference what I felt when I was introduced to someone new who I immediately felt an instant connection and camaraderie with. So, when my son came to me and suggested that I write a book on the subject, I was immediately interested.

This is a book about becoming connected to other people. It is meant to start a conversation and to get you thinking about ways to take your life to another level. This book is primarily for Christians, but non-Christians can also derive benefit from this book. It is my strong belief that no one will ever find true life meaning without being properly connected to God. Having a relationship with God is essential to fully understanding the conversation in this book. Although being a part of any tribe can enhance your life on this Earth and bring you more pleasure and meaning while you are here, it will do very little to help you in the eternal life to come. Being connected to others in a meaningful way is one of the ways that Christ got His message out to others and was put in a position to show others the love and power of God. Evangelism cannot take place without connection.

Hopefully this book will break down some of the

human barriers and prejudices that have plagued humanity for decades, and are gradually getting worse. Hopefully, by reading this book, you will start viewing others, who are not like you, in another way. In my mind, this is a conversation that needs to be started. This is a short-read by intention. In this crazy, fast-paced world, not many have the time for long-reads anymore. If God uses this book to restore even one broken relationship, my prayer has been answered.

Part 01
HUMAN

A TRIBE IS A GROUP OF PEOPLE WHO HAVE A COMMON INTEREST OR COMMON CAUSE.

Chapter 01
THE NEED TO BELONG

Everyone in life has a need to belong. Belonging makes us feel like we matter. It gives us a sense of importance and makes us feel like we can make a difference in life. We can fulfill this need in many ways. We can join a club, become part of a religion, take on a sports team and become a loyal fan, join a car club, join the rodeo circuit, buy a motorhome, become a foster parent, or save the whales. It doesn't matter so much what we do as it matters why we do it. Belongingness is the human need to be an accepted member of a group. Humans have an inherent desire to belong and be an important part of something greater than themselves.

Social psychologists have been studying our need to belong for well over a century. One of the more famous studies on the subject was done by Abraham Maslow in 1943. He suggested that the need to belong was a major source of human motivation and self-actualization. He thought that it was one of eight basic needs. He stated that he had found that after our physiological needs, like our need for food, water and sleep had been met, that the need for belonging was the next step on his hierarchy of needs list.[1]

Paul McCartney once wrote a song about loneliness in a crowd of people. He said, "All the lonely people, where do they all come from? All the lonely people, where do they all belong?" God said in the beginning of the Bible that it was not good for man to be alone. He came up with the idea of marriage and family, and that is kind of where tribal living got its start. God knew that we needed others in our lives in order to experience a sense of belonging and completion.

In November 1992, Donald DeGreve, 65, suffered a fatal heart attack while playing golf in Winter Haven, Florida. His body laid on the 16th green, covered with a sheet, while course officials tried to contact his wife and funeral home personnel. A steady stream of DeGreve's friends, playing in the Swiss Village Mobile Home Park League, passed from the 15th green to the 17th tee to continue their game. "Life goes on," said one man, "so we have to keep going." Now that is a great example of being in a crowd, but not belonging. To live a meaningful life, we must feel like we matter, and that we are part of a group.[2]

In the mid 90's, I was back doing some work in Colorado Springs, Colorado, when I heard on the local news that several men had been skiing down Pikes Peak Mountain, got caught up in some sort of avalanche and all were killed. All the bodies had been rescued except for one. The weather had become so bad that the search for his body could not continue for several days. A friend of the deceased skier was sitting at his desk somewhere back on the East Coast, when he heard the news about his friend, and what had happened. The rescue attempts had to be stopped until the snowstorm passed by. Immediately, he knew what he had to do. There was no way that he could stand the thought of his friend's body having to lay on that mountain for possibly days, because of a storm that had settled in. He left his office job and headed west. In spite of the danger involved and warnings from friends, he hiked up the mountain, braving the storm. He found the body of his friend and called the authorities to come and get them. That is what I mean when I say that we need to belong and be connected to others in meaningful ways.

Human beings excrete neurochemicals, and one such chemical is oxytocin. Oxytocin is a hormone that is produced inside the brain in an area called the hypothalamus. The hypothalamus releases oxytocin and distributes it throughout the body through the blood stream. This oxytocin produces warm, fuzzy feelings in us and serves as a bonding agent. It gives us a "love high." Many who have studied the effects of this body producing chemical are starting to believe it has the potential to not only reduce stress but even counter the effects of stress. It can also help us feel better, sleep better and it has a big effect on our moods. All of this helps us function better in life.

Studies have been done over the years with babies in orphanages. They have found that babies who were in hospitals and institutions that had experienced a lack of human contact were more prone to die of infectious diseases and malnutrition. They simply wasted away in a condition called marasmus. Once these infants were moved out of these institutions and hospitals, where they received little to no personal touch and affection, and placed in loving and nurturing environments with good nutrition and clean surroundings, the marasmus reversed. They actually got healthier, gained weight and began to flourish.

In hospitals all around our nation, they are introducing programs where sick and premature infants are submitted to touch therapy. They are held for 15 minutes, 3 times daily, and the results are no less than amazing. The infants who are being held, massaged or simply rocked by hospital volunteers are growing faster, gaining more weight and leaving the hospital sooner than those untouched counterparts. That is not all. They have also found that volunteer grandparents, who hold these babies and show them affection, are also experiencing significant benefits. We are told that they are experiencing less sickness and disease than others their age. They are healthier, experiencing fewer symptoms of depression and their stress levels are lower than others in their age group.

The point I want to make is that we all need to belong, be close to one another and enjoy the benefits that come from these relationships. I want to talk to you about connecting with others in such a way that we feel like we have a purpose in life. At the same time, we feel loved and connected. We will refer to this connection as "being part of a tribe." As far back as we can remember, tribal association has been part of our primal existence.

People quickly learned over time in the evolutionary process that forming tribes was essential to human success, and oftentimes important for the continuation of existence. In order to protect themselves from invading hostile enemies, they needed to form an alliance. They built and expanded their homes into villages, where all mankind could benefit from interdependent relationships with one another. Tribes were quickly born. We learned that belonging to a bigger and larger group had many benefits, and also gave us a sense of satisfaction and purpose in life.

Things have not changed much today. The majority of us, if not all of us, are tribal people. We have tribal connections, and in many cases are not aware of them. Let me define for you what I mean when I use the word "tribe" in the context of our conversation.

A tribe is a group of people who have a common interest or common cause.

The Need to Belong | 19

They usually have a leader or group of leaders even if they do not recognize the leaders. They also form a group that can be identified by any number of things. They can be identified by a name, colors, ethnicity, bumper stickers, titles, mission statements, memberships, birthplace, among many other things. Let's talk more about tribes.

THERE COMES A TIME WHEN WE HAVE TO BEGIN TO REACH OUT AND FIND OUR OWN TRIBAL ROOTS AND NOT JUST BE CONTENT WITH THE ONES WE HAVE INHERITED.

Chapter 02
SENSE OF PURPOSE

Belonging to a tribe gives you a sense of purpose and identity. It gives you the motivation you need to make it through this journey that we call life. Viktor Frankl, a holocaust survivor, in his book *Man's Search for Meaning* says that a lack of meaning and boredom in an individual's life causes more mental problems than distress. He goes on to say that the lack of meaning and purpose accounts for much of the rise in depression in America.[1]

How big is your world? Do you see the need to extend it? Does it matter to you that every day many people die in the world because of problems that deal with not having enough to eat or not having clean water? I can't even imagine the idea of seeing my child die of hunger. These kids have names, and they really want to have a life, just like our kids do. They want to grow up, get married and have kids. Their parents love them just as much as we love our children. I can't even imagine the pain and grief these parents go through as they watch the children that they are responsible for suffer, and at the same time look to them for provision that they don't have. Does it matter to you that every day somewhere in the world some little innocent girls are being forced into sex trafficking and prostitution? They cry themselves to sleep after being manhandled by some perverted, self-gratifying monster that dares to call himself a human being. Their life has been reduced to nothing more than being a sex object that lives to satisfy the sexual urges of depraved men. The worst pain of all is that some of their parents don't even care. Their parents may be the reason that they are in this predicament.

    Does it matter that some of the elderly in our own country do not have enough money to heat their houses at night? Do all the kids in foster care, who have no one that really cares about them, matter to you? Can you hear their cries and feel their hurt? The pain and suffering in the world cries out to us who have been blessed to help.

    At the end of our days, we need to be able to admit that we had a purpose for being on Earth. We were part of something that made this world a better place and gave meaning to life. At the least, it made our lives more significant and gave us some sense of fulfillment. We can have several different tribal connections in our life, but my wish for us, is that all of us would be a part of some tribe that is helping our hurting humanity.

You say, "But Ron, I am only one person, and I don't have the resources to contribute much. I can't make much of a difference." One day I heard a pastor sharing how he had adopted a child from another country and how this was a passion of his. He wanted others to pray about the idea of adoption. On one occasion right after he had addressed the issue, some overzealous, pragmatist caught the pastor at the door and sought to put things into proper perspective by saying, "Oh pastor, we cannot save the whole world!" The pastor quickly responded, "I don't seek to save the whole world, but this one child." If we would all just do something, even if it is something small, the world would be a better place. If we will only do what we can, it can make a bigger difference than we think.

Tribes unite to make a bigger impact. Many of the tribes exist to help the poor and hurting like the United Way, Salvation Army, Feed the Children, YMCA,

Mayo Foundation, Boys and Girls Club of America, and your local churches. Whatever it is, I encourage you to make it a part of your tribe's mission statement, whether you belong to the local NRA, PTA, the Go-Kart Club of America, or just a local women's group in the neighborhood, to reach out and help the hurting. Show your fellow members a way to do that. I believe that every tribe should give themselves to a charitable cause of some kind and make this world a better place.

When we were growing up, many of us had very dominating but loving parents, whose intentions were good. However, they tried to enforce their purposes for their lives upon us. They just automatically assumed that their purpose in life would also be our purpose in life. They were brought up to believe that it was their job to figure out our lives for us, so they laid out a plan that sometimes included the sports that they wanted us to be involved in, where we would attend school and what our educational major should be. They pushed their religious or atheistic beliefs on us and were sure that we would always believe just like them, but it doesn't always work out this way.

I was brought up in a very religious, father-dominated, uneducated home. I say "uneducated" simply because neither of my parents graduated from high school, and obviously had no college experience either. Because of this, my siblings and I were not even slightly encouraged to pursue higher education. My parents raised me to believe that this was not a necessary part of life. Because my father worked in the oilfields all of his life, he just automatically assumed that I would do the same. At the least, I would just find a blue-collar trade, learn it, stay with it, and make enough money to live a decent life. Nothing more than that ever entered his mind. This was his purpose in life, and he automatically assumed that I would never want anything more than that for my life either.

They got involved in a strict, conservative Christian denominational church, and they made sure that we all lived according to the value structure that was passed on to them through this church. I remember having to go to grammar school on the days that we did square dancing with a note pinned on me that said, "Ronnie isn't allowed to dance, because it is against our religion." We also were not allowed to have a deck of cards in the house, nor could we attend a movie show. We couldn't do any work on Sundays, which included mowing the lawn (that I didn't mind).

Now, I need to interject here that I respect parents who raise their children with a healthy value system. I do think that it is a parent's responsibility to help a child plan for their future, follow house rules and adhere to some form of discipline. It is just unfortunate when we are brought up in a dysfunctional home life. I will say that I do thank my parents for raising me to have a relationship with God, even if it was missing a lot of the major components. I also thank them for making sure that I had a roof over my head and clothes to wear. It could have been a lot worse. My dad also always liked the saxophone, so guess what I played?

My parents did not recognize the fact that God created me to possibly fulfill a different purpose in life than the one they had planned for me. The Bible says that we should raise a child up in the way he should go. In the Hebrew language, it insinuates that we should raise each child up in such a way that we keep their proper bent in mind. Each child will have his or her own disposition and personality. They will be prone to be drawn to different causes and passions because of this bent they were born with. To work against that bent, will not only keep that child from becoming the masterpiece that God created them to be, but it can also lead to that child being a failure in life.

Great parenting requires us to become master craftsmen when it comes to raising children. We all tend to fall into a set pattern of "one size fits all" when it comes to this idea of raising children. Most of us never consider the fact that every child God gives us is created to be a divine masterpiece. We have been given a divine mandate to raise a child that is uniquely made from birth to fulfill a purpose that no one else on this Earth has been assigned to accomplish. We must re-think this whole idea of raising children. We must release them to fulfill the purpose for which they were made. It takes a real mature parent to know the difference between encouraging and mentoring a child to fulfill their purpose in life versus manipulating a child to fulfill our purpose for them.

Many parents believe that they know what is best for their child, without putting any real effort into studying their child's divinely given nature and disposition. This idea scares some parents simply because it requires a degree of loss of control over that child's life, and this doesn't sit too well with some parents. They have never been taught that we are to raise up a child with a weaning process kept firmly entrenched in our mind. We are afraid that they will make a mistake and maybe sabotage their future, leaving the value system behind that we have worked so hard to enforce in their life. They fail to see that if we have done our due diligence in the earlier years by modeling a healthy value system, we have done all that we can do. Now the rest is up to them. Giving advice and continuing to mentor a child all the way into their early 20's and beyond is a healthy thing to do, but so is releasing them to become their own person and accepting them regardless of their choices.

The point I want you to see is that our purpose in life is not always the purpose that we were raised with. There comes a time when we have to begin to reach out and find our own tribal roots and not just be content with the ones we have inherited. The tribes we belong to help us find purpose in life. The Christian tribe I belong to believes in helping the poor, feeding the hungry, healing the broken, as well as showing people how to find God in their life. My particular tribe gives me many opportunities to reach out and become involved in these things. We, as a collective group, built six schools in Ethiopia last year in Muslim villages and supplied them with Christian teachers. Now, some might take offense to the way we are doing this, but it is part of the way my tribe views life. I have a right to belong to a tribe and my tribe has a right to have its own tribal views, just as you have the same right. We must learn to live together, keeping an understanding firm in our minds that different tribes will view life in different ways. No matter how much you disagree with that, it will never change the way things are. It is the way life is. We must learn to agree to disagree and love each other in the process.

BEING IN A TRIBE CAN HELP YOU ACCOMPLISH MORE THAN YOU CAN ON YOUR OWN.

Chapter 03
THE POWER OF CONNECTION

Tribes can help you find your purpose. They can help you broaden the vision of that purpose and help you sustain it. They can help you hook up with others who have a like passion, and who can pool their resources with yours to accomplish some of the purposes of that particular tribe. Being in a tribe can help you accomplish more than you can accomplish on your own. When we pool our resources and work together, our influence becomes greater. Even if you don't think that you need to belong to a tribe, it doesn't nullify the fact that there are many tribes that might need you. We all have been created to help others on their journey in life.

In the Bible it instructs the older women to teach the younger women, and the older men to do the same with the younger men. Tribes help us form connections with others. Those connections become ways of helping others as we share our life experiences with them, pray for them and are there to encourage them when they are down. We all need others in our lives on a constant basis, and tribal connections provide us with these opportunities.

Sometimes we need to force ourselves to be connected to others, or it can become way too easy to become a recluse in life. Again, we get personal value and benefits from putting ourselves in a position to help others. The Bible calls it the "sow and reap" law. What you give out to others, you get back in life. There is almost a selfish part to this. What do you need more of in your life? Peace? Joy? Love? Money? Time? Whatever it may be, you need to put yourself in a position to be able to give that away to someone else. God was ingenious when He created this law of reciprocity.

I came up with an acrostic of HELP for you to remember that you were put on this Earth to help other people. I want you to see that you are a very unique and blessed person, and that there is no one else on this Earth quite like you. Because one of your purposes in this life is to help others, we will use the word "HELP" to show you just what a gift you are on this planet, and hopefully cause you to understand that to keep this gift from others is a very selfish act on your part.

> **H**abits: The good habits that we have, that have helped us become the person we are today, need to be shared with others. Some people don't have the habit of prayer, daily exercise, dieting, etc. These can be infectious if we will allow ourselves to get close enough to people to infect them. We can also use our bad habits to show others what not to do.

> **E**xperiences: We have all been exposed to different things in life, some good and some bad. These past experiences have helped shape us into who we are today. Your past experiences can help other people in a multitude of ways. They can educate people, as well as serve as a warning to them. Your educational experiences, vocational experiences, spiritual experiences, good experiences, as well as your painful experiences can all serve to educate others in your tribe. Your defining moments can add a lot of value to others.

Links: These links and connections to others can help the tribe in a variety of ways. There are times when a tribe needs some of the resources and contributions that only your links with others can provide. Have you ever watched "Celebrity Apprentice"? When it comes time for the "big show" they all call upon their connections with others to pull off an important event. Sometimes very worthy causes cannot become successes without the connections that their members have with other people.

Personality: We all have one. Your personality is the visible aspect of your character as it relates to others. You have a uniqueness about you that exudes from the way you laugh, handle conflict or even see life, that needs to be shared with others. Your personality has been created to be enjoyed by those around you.

Now, let me say something about your personality and how it affects your purpose in life. I think that many of us deal with different sorts of inferiority complexes.

We just don't like to acknowledge some of them. As I talk about getting involved in a tribe, many of us are concerned about how we can fit in. Will they accept me, and do they have a place for me?

I have a firm belief that the ancient Greeks were onto something when they discovered the four basic personality traits. Through most of human history, it has been assumed that people could be classified as having one of four basic personality types or temperaments. The great Greek physician, Hippocrates, made this discovery famous around 400 B.C. (almost 2,400 years ago). He suggested that various amounts of body fluids in each of us had influence over our personalities. For example, some of us have in our bodies more red blood than others. Some have more bile or phlegm than others do, and all of this has a direct influence on how we act and behave.

While Hippocrates' body fluids theory turned out to be a dead-end street, the truth remains that his observation about the human temperaments can easily be observed all around us. I personally can see how there might still be an undiscovered truth that we might be overlooking. To believe that our individual body fluids can influence the way we act is not a far-fetched idea, to say the least. For example, the way I act can really be influenced by my intake of too much caffeine. When I put caffeine in my body, I become nervous, chatty and am ready to go to the gym for a workout. Whereas when I am depleted of caffeine, I am much more reserved and calm in nature. Another example is when I take an Ambien to help me sleep, I act differently than when I am not on Ambien. Any kind of drug that I put into my body usually has an influence on my behavior. I think that you get my point. It just stands to reason that the presence of certain body fluids in our bodies can influence our personalities.

Hippocrates named the four temperaments melancholic, sanguine, choleric, and phlegmatic. There are those who have taken these temperaments a step further and established animal names for them.

> **The Melancholic - The Beaver:** These people are really organized. They have all their shoes lined up in a row in the closet. Their winter clothes are separate from their summer clothes. They are thinkers and doers. They show up on vacation with an itinerary, and if you ever ask them to help you

move, they will spend a lot of time lining up boxes and organizing.

The Sanguine - The Otter: These people are party hardy people. They are usually very social and outgoing, the life of the party. When they show up for vacation, and you ask them if they have the itinerary, they will respond with, "What itinerary? I lost it four days ago." If you ask them to help you move, you have made a big mistake. They will get sidetracked with anything and everything. They will have to try on your old clothes and try the golf clubs out on your front lawn. If they have a term paper due on Monday, they will go to the beach on Saturday. After all, they still have Sunday to study. Today it is time to party hardy.

The Choleric - The Lion: These are your natural born leaders. They don't like to lose, and they tend to be bossy. They are usually charismatic and get things done. When you ask them about the vacation itinerary, they will respond, "We don't need one. I will make it up as we go." If you can't make a decision about something, they will make a decision for you. When you move, they will try to bark out orders to everyone.

The Phlegmatic - The Golden Retriever: These people are very easy to get along with. They are friendly and laid back. They love to serve and are very cooperative. When they show up for vacation and you tell them about the itinerary, they reply, "Whatever you decide is good for me." If you ask them to help you move, then you have made a good decision. While the beaver is busy organizing, the otter is playing and the lion is barking out orders, they are the only ones busy working.

Now, knowing your personality type makes you cognizant of what you have to offer to your tribe. It lets you see your position in that tribe and their need for you. For example, every tribe has a need for organizers (melancholic/beavers), leaders and vision casters (choleric/lions), workers and servers (phlegmatic/golden retrievers), and encouragers, people to promote the tribe to others and make it fun (sanguine/otters). Every tribe needs all of these people. You can never have enough workers, encouragers, administrative people, or leaders to help the tribe grow.

When you go to join a tribe or if you just want to help your tribe to be better, then take a personality test to find out your basic temperament type. Then search for a place to serve your tribe.

Part 02
TRIBAL

STUDIES HAVE PROVEN THAT INTERACTIONS WITH OTHER PEOPLE ARE CLOSELY TIED TO DOPAMINE AND SEROTONIN PRODUCTION.

Chapter 04
TRIBES

Cultural anthropologists usually apply the term "tribe" to a variety of social organizations that are culturally homogeneous, consisting of multiple families, clans and clubs, who share a common language and culture. For our study, we will refer to tribes as those groups of people that we associate ourselves with, which have an effect on the way we see life and also make our life more enjoyable. They can have an effect on the way we see ourselves, and they can help shape who we are becoming, depending on the level that we are involved.

These tribes have the potential to label us, whether we want them to or not. They can influence the way we spend our time, resources and energy, as well as the kind of friends we attract and hang around. Our tribal associations have a huge impact on whom we marry. Some people are more involved in their tribes than others. If we examine our lives closely, we will see that all of us have a tribal nature deep down inside of us that cries out to be recognized.

There is a story about a young boy who was born into a Navajo American Indian family. His dad was full blood Navajo and his mom, who was divorced from his father, was half Navajo and half Cree Indian. One summer morning, this typical American boy was awakened by his father and told to get dressed. He said he was going to take him somewhere. His dad instructed him to pack a bag with a few of his clothes in it and grab his toothbrush. Half groggy and filled with curiosity about where his dad was taking him, the boy obediently got into the car. He asked his dad where they were going, his dad simply said, "Wait, and you will see." They drove for what seemed like a whole day, although it was probably more like five or six hours, until they turned off onto a dirt road high up in the mountains.

They drove on this dirt road for about 30 minutes until they came to a deserted small adobe-like house, with a mud roof and a small barn-like structure in the back. He was now full of anticipation. Out to greet them came an elderly woman of definite Indian descent, who was small in stature and very wrinkled. She looked to be at least 100 years old in the young boy's eyes. His dad greeted the elderly woman with a big hug as she kissed him on the cheek. It was very obvious to the young man that their relationship went back some time. His dad looked at him and said, "Son, I want you to meet your great-grandmother, Grandma Chenoa. I have to go on a short business trip, and I want you to stay here with her for three days. There is something I want her to teach you." The young man, as he looked back on this story, said that his heart sunk with the thought of staying three days in that awful place with that old woman, who had to be near death's door.

The three days passed faster than he had anticipated. His great-grandmother seemed to have no shortage of stories, fully capturing him like nothing he had ever experienced before. She told him stories about the Navajo Nation, about his great-grandfather, and what a great Navajo warrior and hunter he was. She also told him about his great-uncles who fought in the wars, and the acts of bravery that they were known for in the Navajo Tribe. Looking back at the time spent with his great-grandmother, the young man would go on to say,

"I went there that day a typical American little boy, but I left there a Navajo Indian."

The young man had found his tribe. He found something that he could fully identify with; something that gave his life meaning and a sense of purpose. He would never again be the same. That is what being in a tribe is all about.

We all have been created by God to have fellowship with Him. If you choose to believe in the creation account in Genesis, then you will quickly see that in the beginning, we were all created to have fellowship with God. We were not meant to live life in a vacuum. The first man in Genesis was given a wife, a holy teammate. He was then placed in the tribe of God, given a job to do and a purpose to fulfill. Everything went well until he sinned and rebelled. God had to disassociate him with the tribe. Everything went downhill from there. He was tribe-less. He had no sense of purpose, and his family life began to unravel.

Because we all have been created with this empty space deep within us meant to be filled with connection and fellowship by belonging to a tribe, we have been reaching out and trying to fill this void with whatever we can. People belong to groups they can identify with such as clubs, motorcycle gangs, street gangs, the Happy Camper Club, religious groups, Pet Lovers Incorporated, sports groups, save the environment groups, etc.

We put on our bumper stickers. We wear our t-shirts with various slogans. We wear our colors. We get tattoos. We wear cowboy hats, religious garb or anything to inform others that our life is about something more than they can see. We belong. We have purpose. Our life is about something bigger than just ourselves. This is what we were made to do, to belong.

Indeed, the 21st century may be the era when tribes came to be the most influential institutions in the world, according to Orrin Woodward and Oliver DeMille in their book *LeaderShift*. "The groundwork has been laid and the trends are already in play, and nearly every major institution, country, civilization, and nation in the world is made up of many tribes. Many even do not realize that they are part of a tribe, but they are, and their loyalty to these tribes surpasses their loyalty to any other entity."[1]

These tribes have been around for ages. There have been nomadic tribes, agrarian tribes, foraging tribes, informational tribes, technology tribes, industrial tribes, as well as religious tribes. Today, the LGBT (lesbian, gay, bisexual, and transgender) movement has formed a tribe with their leaders and spokespersons. The religious right and the moral majority are also tribes. When we are in another country on vacation, and we see another American, we quickly reach out and want to establish some sort of connection. Why? Because they are part of our tribe.

Without tribes, our lives wouldn't be as meaningful. Productivity would not be at its highest level in many areas of life, and we wouldn't have the power we need to get some things accomplished. Just as the generations of old saw the need to form tribes for the sheer sake of existence and progression in their societies, we do the same today. They give us a venue for sharing our opinions and being part of a voice that can get an audience that might listen. We have a small part, but a part nevertheless. We can boast, "Look what we did!" We belong to that tribe. It gives us a reason to give and also the desire to give. We have a cause that we can give our time and money to. We want our life to be about something meaningful.

Research tells us that generous people enjoy a longer life than those who are self-centered. Jesus knew what He was talking about when He said that it is more important to give than to receive. When we give, our bodies release certain endorphins that make us happier and healthier. Giving affects our brain chemistry. People who give often say that they experience feelings of euphoria. Psychologists refer to this as the "helper high." These helper high endorphins are compared to the sensations that drug users get from heroin and morphine. Giving is not just something you do for your favorite cause, but it is also something that you do for you.

According to the Social Capital Community Benchmark Survey, a survey of 30,000 American households, people who gave money to a charity in 2000 were 43% more likely than non-givers to say they were very happy about their lives. Similarly, those that volunteered were 42% more likely to be very happy than non-volunteers. It didn't matter whether gifts of money and time went to religious organizations or other charitable groups. Givers of all types were far happier than non-givers. Tribal living is a healthy way to live.

A recent study of older adults shows that those who regularly volunteered over the course of five years were half as likely to die prematurely, and it also decreased the amount of depression in their lives. I have always said that motion creates emotion. Some people could do themselves a huge favor (and even get healthier) if they would "tribe-up" and get involved, instead of just lying around and being a couch potato. Just maybe our doctors need to start writing out prescriptions for people to make their world larger.

We were made to make a difference. Some of us live in a very small world that just consists of our immediate family and ourselves. We bury ourselves in meaningless ruts and daily routines that are meant to just pass the time as we grow older by the day. It is so easy to do. We get up in the morning and get ready for work. We eat the same old thing each and every day. We put in our eight hours at work. We go home driving the same route we always do. We get home, sit in the same chair and watch the same old TV shows that we always watch. We go to bed and get up the next day to repeat basically the same routine. On the weekends, we have another routine we put ourselves through, and life becomes drudgery. Then we end up going to see the psychiatrist, because we have fallen into a depression that we can't get out of. With all of their help, we still can't get out of our depression; it only continues to grow worse. Now in some cases, the remedy may be simpler than we have chosen to believe.

We were made for connection. We are tribal people meant to have tribal connections. Have you ever seen an American Indian portrayed in a movie living on a lonely mountainside with one little teepee all by himself? No, you usually see Indians living in a group. It is the way they live. They learned long ago the value of tribal living. There have been studies that have shown that when we have someone to share our pain with, our pain is almost cut in half by the act of sharing. In the same way, when we have someone to share our victories with, our joy almost doubles. Being part of a tribe that views much of life through the same lens as we do usually connects us to people in a more intimate way. It creates relationships where sharing becomes more convenient, easy, and our life becomes fuller in many areas.

Life was meant to be lived, and not just endured. Our predecessors had to live an extreme lifestyle just to exist. They had to fight, hunt and build. They had to always be thinking of how to plan for the future. They lived on their toes with their running shoes on. There was hardly ever a dull moment. God made us for extreme living, not to just sit in front of a computer all day.

I took a college philosophy class years ago, and I remember the professor talking about how there was a profound difference between the way people died who had lived with a purpose and people who died without a purpose. The latter group had a hard time facing and coming to grips with death. They died without much peace in their life. Whereas the other purpose living group was more prepared to die. The Apostle Paul said it best in 2 Timothy 4:6-8, when he said, "For I am already being poured out as a drink offering, and the time of my departure has come. I have fought the good fight, I have finished the course, I have kept the faith; in the future there is laid up for me the crown of righteousness, which the Lord, the righteous Judge, will award to me on that day." Paul had served his tribe well and made his life about purpose.

We were made for extreme living. This is a big reason behind a lot of porn and drug addictions today, as well as many other such vices. Our bodies were made to produce certain endorphins, such as dopamine and serotonin. Although alike in many ways, these two chemicals that act as neurotransmitters are different in the fact that dopamine regulates muscle movement, motivation and the sensation of pleasure. Serotonin primarily affects mood, impulsiveness and social behaviors. Now, the people who are living mundane, boring lives, and not doing the things that promote the activation of these neurotransmitters, are going to feel the impact in their bodies. We need a certain amount of "feel-good experiences" in our lives. We also need a certain amount of excitement and goals that challenge and stretch us. We were made to be participants in life and not just spectators.

God, in His infinite wisdom and knowledge, knew that we would need these chemicals in our bodies if we were to accomplish His will on Earth and live to see the fullness of days. Without these "fight or flight" endorphins, our ancestors would have had their enemies consume them and would have likely starved to death. Our bodies were made to experience a certain amount of activity and extreme living. Now, because some people require more of these chemicals than other people, they participate in extreme sports and are always living on the edge. People who live boring, mundane lives are going to seek out something to fill the perceived absence of these chemicals in their bodies. Some will resort to porn, drug addiction or other such vices in order to find fulfillment in their lives. Obviously, this is not the only reason for the explanation of drug and porn addictions, but it could be one of many.

In the Bible, the Apostle Paul told us to, "Lay aside the old self, which is being corrupted in accordance with the lusts of deceit, and be renewed in the spirit of your mind, and put on the new self..." (Ephesians 4:22-24). The new self was made to live life to its fullest. When we want to fight off a harmful addiction, sometimes there is a need to substitute a good addiction for the bad one. The Apostle Paul compared it to taking off an old, dirty garment and putting on a new, clean one. Substituting something good for something bad is not a new idea. It has been around as long as the Apostle Paul's days.

The new habits we choose should release a certain amount of these "feel-good endorphins" to replace the endorphin rush we were getting from the bad habits. When our body does not have to contend with the absence of these endorphin rushes and its desire to compensate in some way, we will be put in a better place to deal with our harmful addictions. I believe that this is what the Apostle Paul was trying to get across to us. So, if you are fighting a harmful addiction of some sort today, you might want to begin to search for something that you can involve yourself in, something that will bring into your life enough excitement and fulfillment to replenish the endorphins that have been formerly produced by harmful addictions and behavior. This is often the kind of lifestyle that tribes can offer us.

Studies have proven that interactions with other people are closely tied to dopamine and serotonin production. Being social and interacting with others can raise these levels. Fostering and maintaining healthy relationships with others may be one way to help maintain healthy and adequate levels of these neurotransmitters. Tribal connections will definitely provide you with those opportunities. They will also present you with challenging projects, missions and causes that will cause an increase of these endorphins.

An example of this can be found in my own life. I pastor and belong to a Christian tribe of fundamental believers. One of our projects, or "missions" you might say, is to facilitate a booth at the annual Las Vegas porn convention. Our sole purpose is to show these people our love and concern for them by providing them with resources that might help them in their life and spiritual journey. We provide them with books, CD's and brochures that deal with a variety of subjects. We have a prayer request board too. We take their prayer requests, and we send them back to thousands of others to pray over. We are there for the girls who have found this lifestyle to be destructive to their well-being, and we help them find a way out. One of the many driving forces of our tribe is to help people who may be involved in destructive habit patterns. We think that the addiction of porn can fall into that category, but we do it with love and a non-judgmental attitude.

We must understand that these people are part of another tribe, and we must respect their right to be part of any tribe they want to be a part of. We are just there for people who might want to switch tribes. Not all do, but some do.

In my study of the American Indians, I have found that in tribes like the Blackfoot, who usually lived in groups of about 80 to 240 and formed their social structure around bands with each having a respected leader, many in the band were not necessarily blood-related.

They were free to leave one band and join another at any time. This often solved disputes among people who disagreed with their leader. If they wanted, they were free to join another band or tribe that they were more agreeable with.

We have the right to switch tribes whenever we want. I respect an individual's right to have their own tribe, whether they agree with my worldview or not. We will cover this more in the next chapter. What I want you to see here is that substituting one habit for another can sometimes be very beneficial for us. If I am getting a lot of dopamine and serotonin highs from the exhilaration of the good and noble things that my tribe espouses, then I won't feel a need for the things that are destructive to the way that I want to live my life. If I am always filled with these good endorphins, I may not be prone to desire the bad things that produce these same kinds of endorphins. These endorphins are much the same, but the way we can get them differs greatly. Healthy tribal living should provide you with the way and means to get a lot of endorphin rushes and live with a regulated, healthy amount of serotonin levels in your body.

UNHEALTHY TRIBES ARE USUALLY LED BY INSECURE LEADERS, WHO DON'T MIND CAUSING CONTROVERSY OVER PETTY THINGS.

Chapter 05
TRIBAL ASSOCIATION BEGINNINGS

Tribal association can begin as early as grammar school, when we first begin to believe that school is more fun if we belong to a group. Some kids get special attention, because they have been blessed with an ability to learn and catch on to concepts faster than others. They just seem as though they have more brainpower than the other students. Without really being aware of it, they are being introduced into one of their first tribes. They are the "teacher's pets" or the "good student's club." Whatever the title may be, there are definitely tribal roots being grown. They feel like they fit and belong in school. They get special recognition from the chief of the tribe. They feel rewarded for their efforts every time they get a smiley face or a high grade on their test paper. They fit. They belong.

Some of the other students, who have not been blessed with this special brainpower, have ADD or some other reason why they have difficulty learning, feel left out. They usually, either cognitively or not, begin over a period of time to seek out their own tribal identity. They also want to fit in and belong. We must realize just how much this need demands to be recognized. Some join the bullies, the rebellious club, the class comics, or the drug scene, simply because of the need for association. Bullying is a big thing today in the schools in our country. Some students have come to the conclusion that either because of their size, association with other kids or their special strengths, they can intimidate the other children and find satisfaction in doing so. They now belong, and they get a special form of recognition that comes from their peers. Whether good or bad, it makes them feel like they're special.

Some girls who don't fit in may turn to promiscuity in order to feel wanted and appreciated. Other students, as I just said, may turn toward gang association, drug use, sports, or any other number of things that can fill this vacuum in their lives. They need to feel accepted and a part of something bigger than themselves. Those who view porn and use drugs usually find other people who are into the same thing that they are and form a bond. They don't feel alone. In some sort of odd way, these associations help them get through their school years. I think that there is even a "left out group" that tends to band together. These are the quiet kids that don't seem to really identify with the other groups, so they find one another and eat lunch together. Although they may not have as much depth to their association, they do feel that they are part of a group and have value, simply because there are more kids like them.

    These associations and need for tribal identity continue long after our school years have ended. We begin to group together with those around us and form tribes. Some of us join clubs, churches, sports teams, stay-at-home mom groups, senior citizen groups, single's groups, save the environment groups, NRA, activists for LGBT rights, NASCAR, UFC, foster parents, Pet Lovers Incorporated, etc. The point is that we are tribal people by nature. We need a cause. We need a purpose for our lives. We get our bumper stickers, we buy our t-shirts and we find a way to integrate our cause into our conversations with others. Whether it is to save the whales or our religious beliefs, we all feel pretty strongly about our cause and want others to know what we are all about. It's the way we were created.

I am a born again Christian, and I do really feel that everyone should want a relationship with God like I have. However, I do realize that not everyone will. Those are the cold, hard facts. Now, while Christianity is a tribe of a larger tribe we call "religion," it is also broken down into smaller tribes that we sometimes call church denominations. These tribes sometimes fight with one another over church doctrines, creeds, dress codes, and music. Many of us lose sight of the reason for our existence and tribal association to begin with, which is to introduce God to our society. We want people to see the God of the universe, to see a need to have Him in their life and to form a relationship with Him. Unfortunately, we sometimes get so caught up in our own little tribal, petty beliefs that we lose sight of the big picture. I often wonder how we are all going to live in Heaven together if we can't even get along on Earth. It is just a fact of life that we are not going to always agree on some Biblical doctrines found in the sacred scriptures. Some of the greatest theologians in the history of the church could never agree on some of the doctrines that man has held sacred down through the ages. They had to simply come to a place where they agreed to disagree. However, we must do the best we can to agree on as much as we can. The problem with much of the disunity within church tribes has to do with a two-fold cause.

The first cause centers around the erroneous, egotistical idea that any of us are at a place in our life where we are able to say that we are absolutely 100% correct about our view on a controversial subject; a subject that more than likely has been debated for possibly centuries by people who are way more intelligent than we are. To be this egotistical and dogmatic that we assume we understand exactly what the Bible means on a given controversial subject may allude to the fact that we think that someone, with no more intelligence than us, wrote the Bible. All I am saying is that when it comes to subjects and doctrines that are not essential to our relationship with God, we should not allow these differences to come in the way of our love, respect and admiration for one another. After all, we are all part of the same, larger tribe.

I believe the second cause for our problems in this area is because some of the leaders in the church world desire to have the majority of the attention directed towards themselves. They must find contention with their "competition." They somehow believe that belittling and discrediting others will help them build a following. They endeavor to eliminate the competition by nit-picking the differences between them. They know that you need people to build a dynasty. It's the old theory, "If you can't beat the competition, then destroy them." I hold many leaders responsible for much of the Christian tribal wars that are happening today. A tribe's influence and position in society today sometimes has a lot to do with the chiefs who are speaking into the lives of those tribal members. Many tribes have influential leaders at the helm. Healthy tribes are usually led by healthy leaders. Unhealthy tribes are usually led by insecure leaders, who don't mind causing controversy over petty things.

Not all tribes have recognizable leaders. Some tribes are led more by the movement than a leader. But even so, most tribes do have a voice or some sort of influence on those belonging to the tribe. Sometimes these influencers are people, but not always. These influencers can simply be the clubs themselves and their rules, a motto, a brand, a spirit, a driving purpose, or any number of things that draws followers and causes them to unite. The Oakland Raiders tribe is definitely influenced by a dress code and a type of rebellious spirit that comes from the idea of being a part of the "Raider Nation." NASCAR has its bumper stickers, baseball caps and its ties to the redneck culture. There are comedians that make their living by making these associations. There is no one leading spokesperson, but instead there is a spirit that leads the tribe.

TODAY, IN THE COMPUTER AGE, IT IS EASY TO BECOME ISOLATED FROM OTHER PEOPLE AND LOSE CLOSE RELATIONSHIPS WITH OTHERS.

Chapter 06
TRIBAL FELLOWSHIP

Tribes can also provide you with healthy relationships with other people. You will find people in these tribes who are viewing life through the same lens that you are, and you can find fellowship with them. Now the word fellowship comes from the Greek word "koinonia" which means communion, joint participation, sharing, and intimacy. I have referred to it for years as "two fellows in one ship." True fellowship takes friendship to another level. It describes a friendship where you learn from one another and share a common bond. You are yoked together by a mutual interest. This is a great story to illustrate this point.

> *Jean Nidetch, a 214-pound homemaker desperate to lose weight, went to the New York City Department of Health, where she was given a diet created by Dr.*

Norman Joliffe. Two months later, discouraged about the 50 plus pounds still to go, she invited six overweight friends home to share the diet and talk about how to stay on it.

Today, 50 years later, 1,000,000 members attend 250,000 Weight Watchers meetings in 24 countries every week. Why was Nidetch able to help people take control of their lives? To answer that, she tells a story. When she was a teenager, she used to walk through a park where she saw mothers gossiping while the toddlers sat on their swings, with no one to push them.

"I'd give them a push," says Nidetch.

"And you know what happens when you push a kid on a swing? Pretty soon he is pumping, doing it himself. That's what my role in life is - I'm there to give others a push."[1]

Today, in the computer age, it is so easy to become isolated from other people and to lose close relationships with others, except our immediate family members.

Tribal Fellowship | 69

Many of us don't take time out of our busy schedules to be with others, to pour our lives into others and learn from them. In my Christian tribe, the Bible encourages the older people to teach the younger people. It instructs us to spend time together and take care of each other when needs arise. We need other people in our lives. Our tribe puts a huge emphasis on relationships.

It has been said that our overdependence on the computer for knowledge can work against us. Our brain needs time to process a thought in order to retain it. Most of you have probably experienced this before. If you go from site-to-site without pondering and meditating on what you just learned, you will forget it in a matter of minutes. You won't retain that knowledge. Fellowship with others gives you an opportunity to come out of the computer lab and learn from other people in a conversational way. You can ask questions, share experiences and have a lot better chance of retaining knowledge. You can also influence others with some of the things that you have learned. You also bond together and form relationships that will make your life healthier, as well as more enjoyable.

We need to force ourselves to form relationships

with others and to take the time necessary to nourish those relationships, as well as sustain them. They bring great value to our lives. Some things in life that are good for us do not come easy, and tribal membership provides us with the opportunity to form these relationships. Some of them will last for the rest of our life. For Christians, tribal membership paves the way for us to show non-believing people the difference that having God in our life makes. It is a great way for us to form relationships with people that God wants to love and reach out to.

The word "fellowship" in the Greek has in it the idea of sharing resources. For example, if I were in the fishing business with another person, we would share a boat, nets and fishing gear. Why? Because we are in the same business with the same goals. Our purpose is to catch fish, and we have formed a relationship to help us both do that. Somewhere along the line, we felt that we could both benefit if we pooled our resources together and worked toward this common goal. In most areas of life, we can accomplish more when we work alongside others in order to reach a common goal. Where would Apple or Microsoft be at today if they were basically a one-man show, or they were simply a husband and wife team working together out of the house? We can usually accomplish more in a tribe than we can by ourselves.

When we are in a tribe, we unite ourselves with people who have various talents and gifts. For example, one person has good ideas, the other person has vision, another person has money, knowledge, connections, administrative gifts, expertise, or skills. When we work together, we get things done. Usually for a tribe to work, we also have to have leaders and some sort of structure.

When we join a tribe, we must be willing to work with the leadership that is set in place, or get out and find another tribe. We will never find perfect leaders within the tribe. All leadership structures have flaws, but you just need to decide if the value the tribe brings to you is worth some of the flaws that the current leadership brings with it. If you aren't happy with the leadership, speak up and try to make suggestions. We can work with the leadership to try to make positive changes. Don't throw the baby out with the bathwater. Sometimes you have to put up with a few things that you don't agree with in order to get the many benefits that the tribe offers, especially when the benefits greatly outnumber the few things that you are uncomfortable with. Again, we have to agree to disagree.

If you dig deep into the history of the Church of England, you will discover that two of the greatest preachers in the early 18th century were John Wesley and George Whitefield. Although these two great preachers had been close friends at Oxford, they were often in sharp disagreement with each other. Wesley held strongly to Arminian beliefs (emphasizing free will), while Whitefield was a Calvinist (emphasizing predestination). Both men led countless thousands to faith in Christ, but they were at odds theologically. Although Whitefield disagreed with Wesley on these theological matters, he was careful to not create problems in public that could be used to hinder the preaching of the Gospel. When someone asked Whitefield if he thought he would see Wesley in Heaven, Whitefield replied, "I fear not, for he will be so near the eternal throne and we at such a distance, we shall hardly get sight of him."

Part 03
INFLUENCE

WE ALL HAVE OUR RIGHTS AND SHOULD FIGHT FOR THOSE RIGHTS, AS LONG AS THEY DON'T INTERFERE WITH SOMEONE ELSE'S.

Chapter 07
NARROW-MINDEDNESS

Although there are many benefits of belonging to a tribe, there are also a few things that we need to watch out for. As is true with any good thing, there is also a downside. The first thing we need to watch out for is narrow-mindedness. On most every vacation time that I take, I travel around to other churches to see how they are doing things so that I might learn from them. Now, I am well aware that I probably won't agree with many of their policies and practices; after all, they are of a different tribe, but I can still learn from them. If I am not careful, I can get tunnel vision and become so obsessed with my own limited tribal views. I forget that there is a big world out there that is full of wonderful people, with interesting ideas and concepts.

If you study the American Indian culture, you quickly come to realize that many of the tribes had distinct knowledge of how to do certain things that the other tribes could have learned from. If only they would have stopped warring long enough to learn from one another. For example, the Sioux Indians who lived in the Central Plain area of North America lived in tents made from animal hides, called teepee's, while the Navajo Indians have been known to live in six-sided houses that were made of wood and covered with clay called hogans. I am sure that under certain conditions living in a hogan would have benefits over living in a teepee.

The Sioux Indians also had the ability to tame horses and became excellent hunters on horseback. Some of the other tribes could have been more successful hunters if they would have learned from the Sioux Tribe. Many of the tribes learned how to use the resources of the land in distinct ways that other tribes could have benefited from. But not much of this was passed on from tribe to tribe, simply because they were raised to see the other tribe as an enemy or competitor instead of someone that they could learn from.

Today, I don't think that there is a better example of two feuding tribes that can be used to illustrate my point than the Christian Evangelical's war with the homosexual community and vice versa. Not all are involved in this war, but many are. We may not even want to call it a war, but anyone with a spiritual heartbeat knows that it exists. We see many religious tribes, who love to bash and condemn the LGBT community, and many in the LGBT community, who love to condemn the church people for the intolerance they feel, coming from this movement. They do it in their sermons, in their jokes and in their unwillingness to agree to disagree with one another. Most Christians won't get close enough to a lesbian, gay, bisexual, or transgender person to get to know them. It is easy to relegate someone to a life in hell, consisting of pain and torment forever and ever, if you have never really met them, had a cup a coffee with them or felt their struggles and pain.

Many members of the LGBT that I know are some of the most compassionate, kind and caring individuals I have ever met. Do I agree with their worldview or many of their values? No, I do not. My tribe believes that this lifestyle is not one that God is pleased with. Through the years, I have learned some very cool things from people who are committed to the homosexual lifestyle. Some of them have taught me things about love, acceptance and forgiveness that I haven't learned anywhere else. Once I had the courage to come out of my Christian "bubble" and get to know some of these people, my warring disposition began to crumble, and I took on a totally different view of them.

Tribes have coexisted alongside one another for years. Some have coexisted peacefully, and others have constantly been at war with one another. Some have exterminated their enemy tribes with the use of brutal force and violence. Many have never recognized the right of other tribes to exist unless that tribe becomes subservient to them and their desires. We see this kind of tribal war going on in the Middle East at the moment between Israel and the Palestinians, and it has been going on for years. They have not learned to live side by side and agree to disagree.

We all have rights and should fight for those rights, as long as they don't interfere with someone else's. We should always respect other people's boundaries and NEVER try to force anyone to see life our way. They have a right to be the way they are. They can choose to dress the way they want. They can choose to decorate their body in any way they desire. They can choose to talk any

Narrow-Mindedness | 79

way they want AS LONG AS THEIR RIGHTS DO NOT IMPOSE ON SOMEONE ELSE'S RIGHTS. What I don't understand is why we sometimes demand that others see things from our perspective. If they don't, we write them off or at least demote them to a lower status in our life. Why do we demand from others what we are not willing to give ourselves? We sometimes almost demand that people accept us just the way we are, but hypocritically we are not willing to accept them just like they are. It is them who need to be tolerant and not us.

I think that sometimes many of us live with an unsettled fear that to accept someone's right to be different means that we give approval to what they do. Many Christians used to say, "We love the sinner, but hate the sin." Although many used to say that, I really did not see it play out in their lives. We must learn to separate these two things.

We still have too many tribal wars going on today. Some tribes just don't know how to get along with others who are different than them. It is their way or the highway. They hold to the belief that they are the superior tribe; therefore, everyone who does not see life through their lens is somehow inferior and is not worthy of their respect. Some blacks don't accept the whites. Some whites don't accept the blacks. The religious fundamentalists don't accept the LGBT community. The LGBT community won't accept the Religious Right. The die-hard Democrats and Republicans very rarely get along, and the skinheads don't like anyone who isn't white. Gangs claim their territories and refuse to accept one another as fellow human beings.

Now when I say "accept" I am simply referring to giving them the right to be who they are. We don't have to agree with someone's beliefs as being right or approve of their way of life as being correct in order to allow them to peacefully exist in our world without being subjected to persecution or disrespect. We don't have to like their way of life or their way of viewing morality or justice, but the fact remains that they have A RIGHT TO CHOOSE TO LIVE THE WAY THEY WANT. That right needs to be respected by everyone. God has created mankind with the gift to choose.

We don't want to be narrow-minded people nor do we want to be people who don't hold on firmly to our value systems. There are beliefs in my life that are not negotiable at the moment, unless God chooses to divinely

Narrow-Mindedness | 81

show me something different. I have my tribal roots, but I never want to be narrow-minded nor blinded by my ill perceived prejudices either. I want to learn from all people. I believe that a lot of the learning process is centered around our ability and willingness to expose ourselves to other people's worlds and beliefs. We are never through learning. Our exposure to new concepts and ideas has the ability to rearrange our perspectives about life, and they cause us to sometimes reconsider our previous ideas and beliefs.

The following story, Harley Angel, appeared in the newsletter *Our America*.

> *Dodie Gadient, a schoolteacher for thirteen years, decided to travel across America and see the sights she had taught about. Traveling alone in a truck with camper in tow, she launched out. One afternoon rounding a curve on I-5 near Sacramento in rush-hour traffic, a water pump blew on her truck. She was tired, exasperated, scared and alone. In spite of the traffic jam she caused, no one seemed interested in helping.*
>
> *Leaning up against the trailer, she prayed, "Please*

God, send me an angel… preferably one with mechanical experience." Within four minutes, a huge Harley drove up, ridden by an enormous man sporting long, black hair, a beard and tattooed arms. With an incredible air of confidence, he jumped off and, without even glancing at Dodie, went to work on the truck. Within another few minutes, he flagged down a larger truck, attached a tow chain to the frame of the disabled Chevy, and whisked the whole 56-foot rig off the freeway into a side street, where he calmly continued to work on the water pump.

The intimidated schoolteacher was too dumbfounded to talk. Especially when she read the paralyzing words on the back of his leather jacket:

"Hells Angels-California." As he finished the task, she finally got up the courage to say, "Thanks so much," and carry on a brief conversation.

Noticing her surprise at the whole ordeal, he looked her straight in the eye and mumbled, "Don't judge a book by its cover. You may not know who you're

> *talking to." With that, he smiled, closed the hood of the truck, and straddled his Harley. With a wave, he was gone as fast as he appeared.*

The article goes on to say,

> *Given half a chance, people often crawl out of the boxes into which we've relegated them.*[1]

This narrow-mindedness, if not watched over, can even turn into hatred if we are not careful. For example, not too long ago, some Los Angeles Dodgers fans beat a guy up and nearly killed him in the parking lot of the Dodger Stadium simply because he belonged to another tribe. He was a San Francisco Giants fan - at least that was a strong premise for the terrible beating. If we are not careful, we can begin to hate other tribes that aren't like us. I have had other "Christians" express their hatred for me, simply because I don't have ALL of the same views they have. To force or coerce anyone to act against their values is a terrible form of hypocrisy, that no one should wish on another.

We don't want to come to the place where we hate

soccer and everyone who loves it, simply because we are a football fan. We are of the "American sports tribe." We bleed red, white and blue, and some would say that soccer is not an American sport (although, that is now changing at a rapid pace). Some of us hate people who are not our own race. If they are not part of our tribe, then we think they are less human than we are. I am so glad that God is color-blind. Some Hispanic employers only hire Hispanics, and the same is true about some white and black employers. Some of us vote color. It doesn't matter what the candidate stands for as long as he or she is the right color. Some people are highly prejudiced and have never stopped to consider just how stupid that way of thinking is, and how much it has the ability to shrink our world and deprive us of so many blessings. Black or white is just a skin color, and has little to do with what is on the inside.

ARISTOTLE TAUGHT THAT VIRTUE IS THE QUALITY THAT RESIDES BETWEEN TWO EXTREMES.

Chapter 08
SPIRIT OF PRIDE

It is ok to wave your flag, promote your colors and put your bumper stickers on your car, if you keep it balanced. Most of you have seen the cars that are so covered in bumper stickers that your immediate opinion about the person driving is that they are "two tacos short of a combination plate." Aristotle taught that virtue is the quality that resides between two extremes. It is balanced. Although I am told to love the Lord God with all my heart and soul, there is a balancing act to the way that plays out in everyday life.

It has to be relatable. It has to have some earthiness to it. When you become imbalanced, you deter people from your tribe. You do the tribe an injustice by making people think that you are ALL actually a little crazy and imbalanced. Be proud of your tribe and promote it in a good way. After all, there was a reason why you wanted to be involved in the first place. Others might benefit from involvement also if you promote it correctly. It is fine to be proud of your tribe and to want others to want to be a part of it, but don't look down on others who are not a part of your tribe. They have that right.

I saw a Texas Rangers baseball game the other day, and the stands were filled with people with their Texas Rangers hats and t-shirts on. I would assume that many of them had some bumper stickers on their cars. The music being blared over the PA system was mostly country music and had a real Texas flair to it. I am quite sure that these people talked a lot about the Rangers and probably invited their friends to come to the games. They are fans, members of a type of tribe. All that is good and in a spirit of fun, until they start using vulgar language and perverted bumper stickers to promote their animosity. Then, it has gone too far, and they have lost focus. It is ok and even fun to "boo" and applaud to honor our team, but it all needs to be kept in the right perspective.

Within religious tribes, there can be bred a very ugly and destructive form of pride. Some tribes speak in other languages (they call it speaking in tongues). Others baptize in certain names. Some believe that women are subordinate when it comes to certain areas of involvement in the church. Some even hold to the idea that miracles don't exist today and imply, by their actions and attitudes, that people who say they do are either intellectually deficient and/or emotionally unstable. What we need to come to see is that those attitudes are not only immature and born of self-righteousness, but they also go against the very core of what we say we believe in. Unity, love and acceptance are the core of the Gospel message. When it comes to inconsequential differences, we should all learn to get along.

Tribal beliefs run deep. When one tribe tries to change the way that the other tribe views life and their core values, you are going to have a war. Many people have been killed in the name of God. We just don't understand the depth of tribal beliefs and opinions. They run deeper than most people want to believe. Now, that is not to say that we shouldn't challenge the people that we are close with to look at their beliefs and re-examine the validity of those beliefs. It is quite ok to pray that they will change, but it all has to be done in the right spirit and way.

We have the right to stand up and fight for what we believe in when we do it in an appropriate way. However, when the day ends, we must realize that we all have to live in this world together. We are neighbors to one another, we work together, we play on sports teams with one another, we all experience many of the same hurts and pains, and we all belong to the same human tribe. Some day we will all have to answer to God for how we lived our life on Earth, but until then, we must get along. We must accept one another's right to be different than us. The old rock 'n' roll song still carries a well-needed message for us today, when it says, "What the world needs now is love, sweet love. It's the only thing that there's just too little of."

IF YOUR BELIEFS CANNOT STAND SCRUTINY, THEN JUST MAYBE THEY ARE NOT REALLY BELIEFS AT ALL, BUT JUST WEAK OPINIONS.

Chapter 09
LEARNING FROM ONE ANOTHER

Somewhere, somehow, we need to learn to look past the differences and focus on the things that we do agree on. We all want to have good health and make enough money to be able to live a comfortable lifestyle. We want our kids to be in a safe environment, and we long for world peace. We are stuck on this planet together, and we need to all learn to get along. We will never see life exactly in the same way. We need to be humble enough to see that none of us have all the answers to life's difficult questions. We all have a limited view.

     C.S. Lewis said it well when he said, "A proud man is always looking down on things and people; and, of course, as long as you're looking down, you can't see something that's above you."

     I love what Thomas Szasz says about pride and vanity. "Every act of conscious learning requires the willingness to suffer an injury to one's self-esteem; that is why young children, before they are aware of their self-importance, learn so easily; and why older persons, especially if vain or self-important, have great difficulty learning at all. Pride and vanity can thus be greater obstacles to learning than stupidity."

Instead of isolating the people from other tribes, maybe we can learn from them. Maybe we can occasionally ask them to lunch to ask questions about why they believe what they believe. Didn't someone say that we need to seek to understand before we can be understood? We might learn something from them that we never knew before. I wonder why people are so proud of being from Texas. Why do people like NASCAR so much? Why do people care so much about keeping the planet green? We can learn from one another; and who knows, we might want to become a member of one more tribe.

Bill Hybels, in his book, *Just Walk Across the Room*, tells this incredible story that illustrates my point well.

> *Assume the average distance across most rooms is twenty feet - about ten steps. The question I hope to answer is this: What if ten steps - just one one- thou-*

sandth of your daily average - could actually impact eternity?

If so, it might well change the way you walk.

The concept surfaced many months ago after I attended a lunch in a southern state. Hundreds of us representing a variety of ethnicities gathered in a hotel ballroom, and I sensed I was in for an interesting experience. As the rest of my table convened, I would discover that our diversity went beyond race to span age, background, profession, and religion.

The moderator delivered some opening remarks and asked everyone to spend a few minutes before lunch making introductions, revealing where we lived, what we did for work, and why we'd come to the event. As we went through the exercise, I spotted a large African-American gentleman seated across the table from me. During his turn, he introduced himself with a name that was clearly Muslim. Then, half way through the program, he caught my eye across the table and, in the midst of bustling conversations and clinking silverware, mouthed the words, "I love your books!"

Reflexively, I swiveled my head around to see if perhaps a bona fide author had approached our table from behind. Finding no one there, I turned back, dumbfounded, pointed my finger toward my chest, and mouthed, "Me?"

Grinning, he said, "Yes! Let's talk after lunch." Yeah - a dose of intrigue ran through my mind – let's do that.

The lunch progressed while I racked my brain, searching for a rational explanation for how this Muslim man had stumbled upon my distinctly Christian books.

Afterward, he waved me over and began fitting the puzzle pieces together. "I now understand that my comment was probably a little confusing because you assume I'm a Muslim," he said.

> *"I try never to assume anything in situations like these," I laughed, "but yeah, I'm a little curious."*

The man went on to share his story.

> *"It hasn't been an easy go," he said. "As you might imagine, I have had a lot of struggles in social settings. And in my profession we have a lot of cocktail parties and other evening events. The natural pattern for me is to show up fashionably late, graciously accept a drink and something to eat, and throw my efforts into trying to make some business connections. Inevitably, I wind up standing alone, stuck against a wall or isolated in a corner. As soon as I think I've lasted as long as social etiquette requires, I discretely plot my exit and then leave. It is just something that I have learned to live with.*
>
> *"One night, I was at this type of party. As usual, I noticed several small circles of people forming to chat about this or that. I wasn't included, but again, I've become accustomed to the scenario.*

"At one point I saw a man on the other side of the room engrossed in discussion with a few people of his own kind, if you will. Suddenly he looked away from that particular group and noticed me standing alone by the far wall. This is exactly how it happened, Bill. He extricated himself from his conversational clique, walked clear across the room, stuck out his hand to me, and introduced himself.

"You know, it was so easy and natural," the Muslim man continued. *"In the moments that followed, we talked about our mutual profession, about our families and business and sports. Eventually our conversation found its way to issues of faith. I took a risk in telling him that I was a Muslim - I was a little hesitant about how he'd respond. He told me that he was a Christ-follower but that, truth be told, he knew almost nothing about Islam. You can imagine my surprise when he asked if I would do him the courtesy of explaining the basics of Islam over a cup of coffee sometime. Can you believe that? He said that he was a curious type and genuinely wanted to understand my faith system and why I'd devoted my life to it.*

"The next time we met, whatever doubts I had about him truly wanting to hear my beliefs were quickly dispelled. He really sought to understand my life and faith. We began meeting almost weekly, and each time I sat across from him, I was stunned by what an engaged and compassionate listener he was.

"One week, I even took the opportunity to ask him about his beliefs. I'd been a Christian as a kid but had left God, left the faith, left it all because the church my family attended was so racially prejudiced. I wanted no part of that Christianity. When the tables turned and I was on the receiving end of his faith story, he patiently described why he'd given his whole life to this person named Jesus Christ. I couldn't believe how easily the conversation evolved - and how respectfully and sensitively he conveyed his love of God. Despite our deep-seated religious differences, we were becoming fast friends.

"It went on this way for some time as we'd meet to hash through nuances of our faith experiences. Some-

> *times he would ask for a couple of days to find answers to my questions; other times, he knew exactly where I was struggling and seemed to have the perfect words to untangle my confusion. There finally came a day - I remember being home alone when this happened - that I felt totally compelled to pray to God. I kneeled beside my bed, told God everything I was feeling, and in the end gave my life to Jesus Christ. And in the space of about a week, that single decision changed everything in my world! Every single thing."* [1]

Now, the point I want you to focus on is not the fact that a Muslim converted to Christianity, but that one man's interest in another man's life made a strong impact and changed his life forever.

Some people have judged me in the past, without really even knowing what I believed or why I believed it. If your beliefs cannot stand scrutiny, then just maybe they are not really beliefs at all, but just weak opinions. We have a lot to learn from one another. If we would just be courageous enough to lay down our tribal prejudices and seek to be interested in other people, we can discover why they are the way they are. Even if we don't agree

Learning From One Another | 101

with their life views, it will help us understand them and accept them for who they are. Everyone has a right to live their life the way they want without us having to agree with them.

Jesus taught us to love even our enemies. That, my friend, is a tall order, but one we should endeavor to fulfill. I desire for everyone to have a relationship with God like I do, but as I have already stated, I realize that no matter how much I desire everyone to have this life that I have found, it just won't happen. I am called to share the good news of the Gospel with everyone. But for those who do not desire a life with God, they at least can become a part of a tribe that will make this Earth a better place to live and learn to get along with others.

As I said in the beginning, most all of us belong to a tribe of some sort. Maybe we are loosely connected, but there is something we identify with at some level. It shows up all the time in our conversations: "You are an American, so am I." If you are a Christian, a Mormon, a baseball fan, a foster parent, an animal lover, own a motorhome, a hunter, a fisherman, an environmentalist, a cowboy, a single person, a body builder, or a senior citizen, there are a lot more of you out there. The more connected you are, the more tribal you become.

These groups can all be broken down into smaller tribes. The smaller the tribe, the better connection and the more benefit you will derive from it. The smaller tribe helps define you more than the larger one does. Many of you just have not made the connection yet. Tribal connections are good for you in many of the ways I have mentioned if you use them in the way God intended for you to use them, and make sure that they are tribes worthy of your time and involvement. If you feel as though you are tribeless, then maybe it is time to start looking around to see all the benefits that you can derive from being in a tribe.

Part 04

YOU

WE CAN'T CHANGE PEOPLE, BUT WE CAN LOVE THEM AND SHARE OUR LIVES WITH THEM.

WE LEAVE THE REST UP TO GOD.

Chapter 10
WHAT TO LOOK FOR IN A TRIBE

Because I am a Christian person who has a strong commitment to the Bible and what it teaches, my search had to begin there. In the beginning, I saw a lot of religious tribes right away that I knew I didn't want to be a part of. I would look at them and say, "I don't know a lot about Christianity yet, but what I do know is that I don't want to be a part of that." I saw some "Christians" living such self-righteous lifestyles, bashing others that were not part of their tribe, fighting over inconsequential creeds and doctrines, and talking more about what they were against than what they were for.

The lifestyle they were advertising did not appeal to me in the least. I did not see them looking anything like the Jesus of the Bible. I didn't really care if they were a Democrat or a Republican, nor did I care if someone drank a can of beer or had a far-fetched view of Heaven or Hell. I just cared about helping broken people get fixed, and I felt that having a relationship with God would put them on a journey toward restoration. I wanted to live more like Jesus than the way that many of these religious people were living. I had a longing in me for a more radical, nonconforming, in-your-face love for people, than what I was seeing in their movements.

Jesus was seen as a heretic in His day and age. A "heretic" is basically someone who holds controversial opinions, especially one who publicly dissents from the officially accepted religious dogma of the day. Jesus challenged a lot of things that the religious people of His day held as sacred and holy. He was seen as a heretic in His day, no doubt about it. So much so, that the RELIGIOUS PEOPLE had Him killed. Now, Jesus gave His life for something that He believed in, and something within me cried out to be identified with a belief system that resonated so deeply that someone would die for it. Not many people that I know ascribe to a belief system that runs that deep.

At the time I was searching for God, the idea that Jesus would die for something He believed in drew my curiosity. Why would anyone die for what they believed in? Why not just change your beliefs or alter them a bit? Because I had been raised in a religious environment, I was also intrigued by how Jesus was willing to stand up to the religious leaders of the day and challenge many of the hypocrisies that they had adhered to in the name of God.

As I learned more, I came to the conclusion that I wanted to identify with Him, and not the religious movements I saw all around me. I think that the religious movement of our day needs to be challenged. Many of the tribes within the ranks of "Christendom" are always fighting with one another over the most petty and ridiculous things. As I stated in *Polyester People* that I wrote some years back, a major religious tribe once sent out mailers throughout the nation asking all Christians to boycott Disneyland because they hired "gays." HOW ABSURD AND HYPOCRITICAL IS THAT? Why not just boycott every corporation and business that hired anything but Christians? I thought that Jesus taught us to love those that we disagreed with.

I eventually had to start my own tribe. I prayed and waited until I felt that I received permission from God to start my own Christian tribe. Now we are a Christian tribe and do adhere to all the basic precepts of the Word of God as we understand them to be. We are a basic, Bible believing tribe that seeks to honor God in all we do and say. There are many more tribes like us, and there are many that are not like us. We are different from some other Christian tribes in the way we view other people that are not a part of our tribe. We do not view them as the enemy, but people that God loves and sent His Son to die for. One of the big ways that we differ from many tribes around us is in the way we relate to these other people. We believe in integration and not separation. We are not afraid of getting our hands dirty nor are we afraid of meeting these people where they are at, regardless of how the religious community may frown on what we do. Jesus was called "the friend of sinners."

As I mentioned before, we facilitate a booth at the annual Las Vegas porn convention every year. At our church, we gather over 1,000 people to serve our city 2 times per year. We have Sundays where we offer free haircuts and fix kids' bikes. We have even given money away in the offering plates before. We have a group of women in the church that regularly visit the strip clubs with gift baskets in hand to show the girls that we care about them. We even helped one stripper move and find furniture for her little apartment. We never tell these women that we approve of what they are doing, but we do believe that many of these women can be healed from some of their brokenness through simply being shown that they are worthy of God's love.

We don't love to convert; we love just because that is what God has instructed us to do. If there are any conversions, then that is up to God. We can't change people, but we can love them and share our lives with them. We leave the rest up to God. We think that this is the way Jesus lived. He touched people with God's love and His message, and then moved on. We also support a group of people who regularly visit our city's prostitutes and love on them in the same way that the stripper ministry I have described operates.

Our Easter services in the past have operated more like a Las Vegas show than a religious event. We have had dancers, performers and people who have appeared on *America's Got Talent* and *Saturday Night Live*. We have had Beatles and Elvis impersonators, DJ's, tap dancers, and even college marching bands and cheerleaders. One of our tribe's most important mission statements centers around telling people how great our God is. What better way to present that message to them than throwing a great big party on Easter and inviting them to it? Everyone likes parties. In the middle of the party, we get to share the reason for why we believe.

Now, other Christian tribes do it differently, and we do not criticize them for that. We hope that they don't criticize us for what we do. We have some practices and ways that some other Christian tribes may not like nor appreciate, but that is ok. That is the idea of tribal living. We won't always understand the ways of the other tribes. The point I want to make is that when we are looking for a tribe to become a part of, the first thing we look for is a tribe that lines up with our worldview and value system; one that is about what we want our life to be about.

The next thing that we look at is the requirements that the tribe has for their members. If they are too stringent, then you might want to run. There have been religious sects over the years that have made you give up all your relationships with others that weren't part of their tribe, and forced you to get their permission before you made any major decisions in life. We call these tribes "cults." Stay away from them. Many tribes do have some set of rules and by-laws, but they need to be reasonable and fit the tribe's mission statement.

Another thing we need to look for is how much time and involvement it will take to be a part of that tribe. How many meetings and functions do they require us to attend? At what level does our commitment have to be? Can we sustain that level, or do we even want to?

Lastly, what kind of reputation does that particular tribe have in the community or nation? Now, not everybody will have nice things to say about every tribe and what they stand for; if there is too much negative sentiment about the tribe, then you might need to look further. Again, always consider the source of the negativity. Other tribe members may want you to become part of their tribe; therefore, they may have nothing good to say about the tribe that you are inquiring about.

THE MOST PRIMAL OF ALL TRIBES IS THE HUMAN TRIBE.

Chapter 11
REACHING OUT AND BRIDGING THE GAP

There are times when we need to embrace people from other tribes. It is a beautiful thing when this happens. There is a story told that has several different versions to it about Jackie Robinson, who was the first black person to ever play major league baseball. Breaking baseball's color barrier was no easy chore. Wherever he went, he faced jeering crowds. There were boos and insults being hurled from the fans in almost every city he played in. One day while playing on Cincinnati's Crosley Field, Robinson endured racial taunts, jeers and death threats that would have broken the spirit of a lesser man. He stood on first base with his head down, humiliated while the fans booed. That is when shortstop Pee Wee Reese, captain of the Brooklyn Dodgers, called for a time out. Reese was a white man from the south, who at that time and place would have been the last person anyone would expect to do anything for Robinson. He walked over to Robinson, reached out and put his arm around him. Together they faced the crowd. The fans grew quiet. Later on, Robinson said that the arm around his shoulder saved his career.

That is something that speaks truckloads to many people, and serves as a shining example of how people from other tribes should react towards one another. We don't have to be from the same tribe to reach out and love one another. I don't agree with a lot of things that other tribes stand for. I also don't want my children or grandchildren espousing some of the more radical views of other tribes, but that should not keep me from reaching out to them and loving them in spite of our differences. The most primal of all tribes is the human tribe. We can all relate to the everyday hurts and pains that come from just being alive on this planet, and we need to help each other along the way as we see a need, without considering tribal differences.

I once heard of an ingenious plan a school administrator came up with in order to bridge the gap between the racial and economic divide in a racially diverse school. He had all the kids come out to the football field and stand in a straight line. He then began to ask them to answer a series of questions. He first asked how many kids lived in a broken home. On these students, he placed a blue dot on their clothing. He then asked the students who had ever been so embarrassed by their lack of nice clothing that they didn't even want to come to school to raise their hands. He placed a red dot on the front of their clothing. He then went on to ask how many of the students ever felt lonely and depressed, and he placed a yellow dot on them. Then he asked how many had ever contemplated suicide, even for a moment, or had ever felt unloved by their parent or parents. He identified them with another color. How many had ever been bullied? After a series of questions like these and placing corresponding various colored dots on the students, he then challenged the kids to look around at the other students.

    He wanted them to see that no matter what color they were or what economic or social background they came from, they were all battling something. In reality, they were all alike in many ways. The point was made. He gave them a word picture that some of them would never forget. They needed to work harder at accepting one another.

    A lot of people with deep tribal roots walk around

with a chip on their shoulders. We need to all dedicate ourselves to becoming initiators in breaking down some of these walls. When we see a need, we should go out of our way to try to meet it regardless of the person's race, sexual preference, political persuasions, or economic status. I think that this is a bigger problem than society chooses to acknowledge today. If some of us were honest with ourselves, we would see this idea of preference and partiality being played out in our lives in practical daily living. Deep in our subconscious minds, I am not even sure that we are cognizant that they exist.

Take for example, a nicely dressed person in their newer SUV in the Costco parking lot struggling to get a rather large and awkward chair they just purchased into their car. Would most of us stop and help? I would think so. But tweak that same scenario a bit, and make it where we see a rather poor looking person, possibly of another ethnicity than ourselves, tattooed out and struggling to get the same chair in a car that's missing a bumper, with a two-tone paint job. I would venture to say that less of us would stop, simply because the person wasn't part of our tribe, either economically or quite possibly racially. Our minds have been trained to recognize the people we can relate to.

    Like it or not, we are not quick to embrace people that are not like us in some way. We are quick to return a smile when an attractive person of the opposite sex smiles at us in the upscale shopping mall, but then we don't even make eye contact with the maid at the hotel where we're staying, to even know if she was smiling or not. We might hold a door open for elderly people or people much like ourselves when out, but not so much for a teenager, who looks like they just jumped off a page of some punk rock magazine. Most of us "deeply religious people" would never dream of going to lunch with someone who was openly a member of the LGBT community. Most of us pick and choose whom we are going to relate to and how we will relate to them, based on our tribal roots and upbringing. When someone begins to break this cycle, it is so refreshing to see.

NO MATTER HOW MUCH WE PROTEST AND ARGUE OUR CAUSE, THE DEEP-ROOTED TRIBAL BLOOD OF OTHERS IS GOING TO KEEP THEM FROM SEEING LIFE OUR WAY.

Chapter 12
THE THREE LEVELS OF TRIBES

There are basically three levels of tribal living that we can be associated with. Level one is core tribes, level two is comfort tribes and level three is choice tribes. The "core tribes" are those tribes that we choose to be a part of that add such deep meaning to our lives, that they even begin to play a big role in defining who we are and who we are becoming. These tribal roots are so deeply ingrained in us that sometimes we feel as though we were predestined to be a part of this tribe. We tell ourselves maybe we were born for this purpose. Some of these tribes can center around our religious beliefs, non-religious beliefs, racial status, sexual identity, political disposition, philosophy of life, love for animals, or even our love for the environment, just to name a few. At this tribal level, we feel that we were somewhat preordained to live this way. This is the level where we would usually rather fight than change. We can also become very argumentative and defensive when anyone challenges us on anything to do with our tribal views. This is also the area of tribal living that society needs to start talking about.

We must become a nation who begins to understand that at this level, no matter how much we try to sell our cause and views to others, not everyone is going to buy into our way of seeing life. Not everyone is going to love the whales, want to save the environment or appreciate our religious views like we do. Not everyone is going to think that our sexual preferences are ok. No matter how much we protest and argue our cause, the deep-rooted tribal blood of others is going to keep them from seeing life our way. We must learn to agree to disagree and deal with all the hatred and strife, as well as frustration that we are causing by insisting that our views be accepted by others.

Now, it is ok to lobby our causes in a right, civil and loving way, but once we see the first sign of bitterness and resentment against those who are of another disposition and tribe, we must acknowledge that we are losing focus and becoming an embittered person. Not everyone is going to see life the way we do. We are all looking at it through a different lens. Yet, we have these leaders of our tribes who at times insist that with enough effort, we can persuade society at large to see life our way. That is simply unrealistic, and it causes a lot of needless dissention in the world. Gaining new converts to our tribe is what most of us desire, but it has to be done in the right way.

We need to learn to accept one another as fellow human beings that have a right to choose to see life differently than us, and we need to do it WITH A SMILE. Besides, haven't we ever learned that we can cause people to turn a deaf ear to what we espouse as truth, by the disposition in which we present it? Our attitudes speak a lot louder than we think. Show me a movement that lacks love and understanding, and I will quickly show you a movement that I have to keep myself from getting bitter against. On the other hand, show me a movement that is patient and kind in its approach to other tribes, and I will show you a movement that I might be open to hearing more about. This doesn't mean that you can't have beliefs and convictions that are incongruent with others and that you can't have distinctly different views than others have; it just means that you carry these differences in a spirit of love and understanding. Listen to this true story.

Rabbi Michael Weisser lived in Lincoln, Nebraska. For more than three years, Larry Trapp, a self-proclaimed Nazi and a member of the Ku Klux Klan, directed a torrent of hate-filled mailings and phone calls toward Weisser. Trapp promoted white supremacy, anti-Semitism and other messages of prejudice, declaring his apartment the KKK state headquarters, and himself the Grand Dragon. His whole purpose in life seemed to be to spew out hate-ridden racial slurs and obscene remarks against Rabbi Weisser and all those like him.

At first, Rabbi Weisser was so afraid that he locked his doors and worried himself sick over the safety of his family. But one day, Rabbi Weisser found out that Trapp was a 42-year-old clinically blind, double amputee. And he became convinced that Trapp's own physical helplessness was a source of the bitterness he expressed. So Rabbi Weisser decided to do the unexpected. He left a message on Trapp's answering machine, telling him of another side of life…. a life free of hatred and racism. Rabbi Weisser said, "I probably called ten times and left messages before he finally picked up the phone and asked me why I was harassing him. I said that I would like to help him. I offered him a ride to the grocery store or the mall."

Trapp was stunned. Disarmed by the kindness and courtesy, he started thinking. He later admitted through tears that he heard in the rabbi's voice, "Something I hadn't experienced in years. It was love." Slowly, the bitter man began to soften. One night he called the Weissers and said he wanted to change, but didn't know how. They went over to his house and took him dinner. Before long, they had made a trade: in return for their love, he gave them his swastika rings, hate tracks and Klan robes.

Very soon after, Trapp gave up his Ku Klux Klan recruiting job and dumped the rest of his propaganda in the trash. "They showed me so much love that I couldn't help but love them back," he finally confessed.[1]

That, my friend, is the way it should be. If our cause is as great as we say it is, then we need to show the love of God to others instead of ranting and raving about why everyone should see things our way.

Level one core tribe values run deep. People can change the way they live, but it will usually only come when someone prays for them and shows them God's love. Theodore Roosevelt said, "Nobody cares how much you know, until they know how much you care."

Level two tribal living is what I call "comfort tribes." These are smaller tribes that help define the larger tribes and break them down into smaller components. Not everyone ascribes to all of these different levels of tribal living. Let me give you an example. As I said earlier, I am a born again Christian. That is my core tribal association. But because there are so many "Christians" out there with varying beliefs that concern many smaller areas of Christianity, I felt led to join a smaller, more defining movement that better proclaims who I am. Some people refer to these as "church denominations." We don't use that word, but just identify ourselves by our name: Valley Bible Fellowship or VBF. Some call themselves "VBF'ers." Now, when you mention our name in and around our community, most people readily know what we are about. We are part of the Christian church that lives on the radical edge a bit more than others do.

We are, for lack of a better way to describe us, a part of the Christian church that makes living for God more about the practicality in everyday life. We don't see a need for a lot of religious ceremonies and traditions. I needed to have the comfort that comes from this less liturgical approach. For others, it is just the opposite. For the Catholics, this decision could entail whether I become a Maronite Catholic, Byzantine Catholic, Charismatic, or an Orthodox Catholic. Those groups can even be broken down into different parishes. The idea of the comfort tribe is to make you more comfortable with your core tribal beliefs. Many of the core tribal beliefs have too much of a wide scope, they need more clarification and a slimmer focus. These smaller associations do this for you.

Last is what I call "choice tribes." These can be easier identified as hobbies, clubs and associations that you join up with and become a part of. They give your life more meaning, and they are enjoyable. They don't have to be even remotely connected to your core and comfort tribes. You choose these tribes for any number of reasons. You might join up because you are bored or you just enjoy the things these tribes are about. For example, I like hunting and almost any kind of sports. I am a Los Angeles Dodgers fan and a San Francisco 49ers fan. I bleed blue in the spring and summer, and I like the red and gold in the fall and wintertime. We don't like Raiders fans or the Giants fans, but we keep this dislike light-hearted. We are a loyal tribe, and when we see someone wearing our colors, we have this automatic bond and mutual feeling for one another, and we can start a conversation without even really trying. These choice tribes can be changed often, and they are not nearly as deeply rooted as the other two tribal levels.

WE ALL BASICALLY WANT THE SAME THINGS IN LIFE.

WE WANT TO BE LOVED, ACCEPTED AND WE WANT TO FEEL THAT OUR LIVES MATTER.

Chapter 13
MAKING THE WORLD A BETTER PLACE

The main point I want you to see is that we must all learn to get along. I believe that being knowledgeable about some of these things that I have mentioned will help get us to a place where we can do that. We need to lay our weapons down, love one another, seek to understand one another, and most of all agree to disagree. We will all stand before God someday and give an account for our lives, but until then, we need to turn our attention to hurting humanity. We need to let our energy be focused not on what we disagree about, but what we do agree about. I will never stop praying for people to come into a loving relationship with God. I will also loudly proclaim that what the world needs most today is a personal relationship with Jesus. But, if people choose to live a different way, I will not treat them any differently than I do anyone else. I will respect their right to be different than me. Most of all, I will love them the best I can and treat them as a member of my most basic tribe, and that is being a part of the human being tribe.

We all basically want the same things in life. We want to be loved, accepted and we want to feel that our lives matter. If there is a God out there, we want to be on His good side. We want to have enough money to meet our needs and fulfill our basic desires. We can relate to one another on those things. That is being a part of the human tribe.

> *In 1873, a Belgian Catholic priest named Joseph Damien De Veuster was sent to minister to lepers on the Hawaiian Island of Molokai. When he arrived, he immediately began to meet each of the lepers in the colony in hopes of building a friendship. But wherever he turned, people shunned him. It seemed as though every door was closed. He poured his life into his work, erecting a chapel, beginning worship services and pouring out his heart to the lepers. But it was to no avail. No one responded to his ministry. After twelve years Father Damien decided to leave.*

Making the World a Better Place | 131

Dejectedly, he made his way to the docks to board a ship to take him back to Belgium. As he stood on the dock, he wrung his hands nervously, recounting his futile ministry among the lepers. As he did he looked down at his hands, he noticed some mysterious white spots and felt some numbness. Almost immediately he knew what was happening to his body. He had contracted leprosy.

It was then that he knew what he had to do. He returned to the leper colony and to his work. Quickly the word about his disease spread through the colony. Within a matter of hours everyone knew. Hundreds of them gathered outside his hut, they understood his pain, fear, and uncertainty about the future.

But the biggest surprise was the following Sunday. As Father Damien arrived at the chapel, he found hundreds of worshippers there. By the time the service began, there were many more with standing room only, and many gathered outside the chapel. His ministry became enormously successful. The reason? He was one of them. He understood and empathized with them.[1]

Most of us live in a very small world; many of our ideas are preconceived and quite possibly based on some level of misconception. I know that there are people who don't understand why I believe what I believe, and why I hold so tenaciously to my worldviews. Some have formed an opinion about me simply because they have never taken the time to get to know me.

I was having dinner with a guy some time back who looked at me, and simply said, "I want to ask for your forgiveness. I really had you figured out to be someone different than you are." Now, I realize there might be some people that when they get to know me, might still hold me at arm's length because of my tribal views. In this case, it was a lack of knowledge and false information on me that caused this guy to dislike me and form a negative opinion about me. Sometimes we need to try to see life from the other person's perspective in order to truly understand them. There might be a great explanation as to why they are inclined to be the way that they are, that will help us understand how to pray for them and accept them.

Through the years, I have read many books and heard many sermons encouraging parents to show outward affection to their children like hugging them and saying the words, "I love you." Now, even though I knew that this was a necessity for a healthy family life, I still struggled with actually doing it. There was a reason behind my struggle that made me the way I was.

When I was growing up I had a verbally abusive father, who on many occasions would verbally abuse me in front of my teenage friends. A classic example of how this happened repetitiously could be summed up in this way: Three or four of my friends would be at my house discussing plans for the weekend or just hanging out when something would tick my dad off. He would unleash a three or four minute verbal tirade toward me. These friends, with a fearful look on their face, would disperse rapidly saying something like, "See you later, Ronnie." Usually within 15 minutes my dad would cool down and call me into the room, try to hug me and tell me that he loved me. From my perspective, that hug could not undo the damage of extreme humiliation and embarrassment that had already occurred.

Needless to say, I came to a place where I associated hugs and the phrase "I love you" with something that brought back bad memories for me and made it difficult for me to do with my family. Now I agree that as adults, we need to mature to a place where we get healed from our childhood abuses and neglect, but it isn't always easy. Maybe instead of judging the stripper living next door or the abusive angry guy at work, we should try to get to know them better. Maybe we should invite them to lunch and ask to hear their story. We might be surprised. We might actually stop "tolerating" them, and start feeling love and compassion for them.

Before we pass judgment on anyone else, we need to put ourselves in their place and see how the problem looks through their eyes. Until we see both sides, we are not fit to pass judgment. Things may look quite differently through your neighbor's window.

> *A well-known Ohio judge was noted for his defense of slavery. He was converted from the error of his ways by the following conversation with a runaway slave, who had crossed the Ohio River from Kentucky.*
>
> *Judge: "What did you run away for?"*

> *Fugitive: "Well judge, I wanted to be free."*
> *"Oh! Wanted to be free did you? Bad master I suppose?"*
> *"Oh, no; very good man, master."*
> *"You had to work too hard then?"*
> *"Oh, no; fair day's work."*
> *"Well, you hadn't a good home?"*
> *"Hadn't I though! You should see my pretty cabin in Kentucky!"*
> *"Well didn't you get enough to eat?"*
> *"Oh, yes, sir. Plenty to eat."*
> *"You had a good master, plenty to eat, were not overworked, a good home. I don't see what you wanted to run away for."*
> *"Well, judge, I left the situation down there open. You can just go down and get it."*[2]

The man had a good reason for being like he was and wanting to be free. It was just the judge's lack of understanding that stood in the way.

I have my reasons why I view life the way I do. I do believe that someday we will all stand before the judgment seat of God, and have to answer for how we lived our life on this Earth. I believe that the Bible is God's Word and that a wise person will study it to see how God expects us to live, but until that time, we all need to try to get along.

General Robert E. Lee was a devout follower of Jesus Christ. It is said that soon after the end of the American Civil War, he visited a church in Washington, D.C. During the communion service, he knelt beside a black man. An onlooker said to him later, "How could you do that?" Lee replied, "My friend all ground is level beneath the cross."

I hope that this book has helped you in some way. It was meant to be a conversation. It was not meant to give you all the answers, but to get you to start thinking and asking questions. My desire is that people would put a little more effort into why they believe what they believe, and learn to love others in spite of those beliefs. It would make the world such a nicer place to live.

NOTES

Chapter 1: The Need to Belong

1. Abraham Maslow. "Theory of Human Motivation," *Psychological Review*, 1943. Web. September 2013. <http:// psychclassics.yorku.ca/Maslow/motivation.htm>.

2. Associated Press. "Golfer Suffers Fatal Heart Attack, but Group Asked to Play Through," *Los Angeles Times*, 16 November 1991. Web. September 2013. <http://articles.latimes. com/1991-11-16/sports/sp-1508_1_heart-attack>.

Chapter 2: Sense of Purpose

1. Viktor E. Frankl. *Man's Search for Meaning* (Boston, MA: Beacon Press, 2006).

Chapter 4: Tribes

1. Orrin Woodward and Oliver DeMille. *LeaderShift* (New York, NY: Hachette Book Group, 2013).

Chapter 6: Tribal Fellowship

1. Richard Innes. "Weight Watchers," *ACTS International*, Web. October 2013. http://www.actsweb.org/articles/article.php?i=1028&d=2&c=6.

Chapter 7: Narrow-Mindedness

1. Craig Brian Larson. "Harley Angel Story," *750 Engaging Illustrations* (Grand Rapids, MI: Baker Books, 2007) 275.

Chapter 9: Learning from One Another

1. Excerpt taken from *Just Walk Across the Room* by BILL HYBELS. Copyright © 2006 Bill Hybels. Used by permission of Zondervan. www.zondervan.com

Chapter 12: The Three Levels of Tribes

1. Manny Fernandez. "Lessons on Love, From a Rabbi Who Knows Hate and Forgiveness," *The New York Times*, January 4, 2009.

Chapter 13: Making the World a Better Place

1. Author Unknown. "Incarnation," *Nelson's Complete Book of Stories, Illustrations, & Quotes* (Nashville, TN: Thomas Nelson, 2000) 258.

2. M.R. DeHaan and H.G. Bosch. "Take Your Neighbor's Place," *Our Daily Bread: 366 Devotional Meditations* (Grand Rapids, MI: Zondervan Publishing House, 1959) January 22.

ABOUT THE AUTHOR

RON VIETTI
Pastor Ron Vietti is currently the Senior Pastor at the church he and his wife, Debbie, pioneered almost 40 years ago in Bakersfeld, CA. Learn more about VBF Church or to hear Pastor Ron Vietti speak live, tune in online at **www.vbf.org.**

CONNECT

BLOG
ronvietti.com

TWITTER
@ronvietti

FACEBOOK
facebook.com/pastorronvietti

LIVE
vbf.org

READY TO BUILD YOUR TRIBE?

nCourage Media is looking for people like you. If you have a book idea, a blog, a film idea, or you just need some media advice, we want to hear from you.

You were made for a purpose, and that purpose is now. If you are interested in finding out more, please visit **nCouragemedia.com.**